GILBERT & SULLIVAN

Arias for Flute and Piano

Arranged for
SIR JAMES GALWAY

by
DAVID OVERTON

CONTENTS

FOREWORD

I first came across the wonderful Gilbert & Sullivan operettas when, many years ago, I played in the Sadler's Wells Opera orchestra, which later became the English National Opera.

I often equate playing the flute to singing, and I love good tunes, with which the G&S operettas abound. So, it's not surprising that in conjunction with my arranger David Overton, I should choose to compile an album of some of the songs.

I have not included songs which, like the 'patter songs' are particularly dependent on the wit of Gilbert's words, but rather on those where the beauty of the melody is such that I don't see why we cannot take advantage of them just as the singers do!

Some of the songs are best suited to solo flute and piano, some for two flutes and piano, and some lend themselves to a flute choir, repertoire which I know is always welcome, and we have separated the arrangements in to separate albums for these three categories.

I hope you will enjoy playing them as much as I do. I often find it suits the flute to play the melody line up an octave – for example in "A Wand'ring Minstrel I "– and I leave you to do the same if you wish.

Sir James Galway

A Wand'ring Minstrel I

from *The Mikado*

arranged for Flute and Piano

for Sir James Galway by

David Overton

Sir Arthur Sullivan

B577

4

On a Tree by a River

"Willow, tit-willow"
from *The Mikado*
arranged for Flute and Piano
for Sir James Galway by
David Overton

Sir Arthur Sullivan

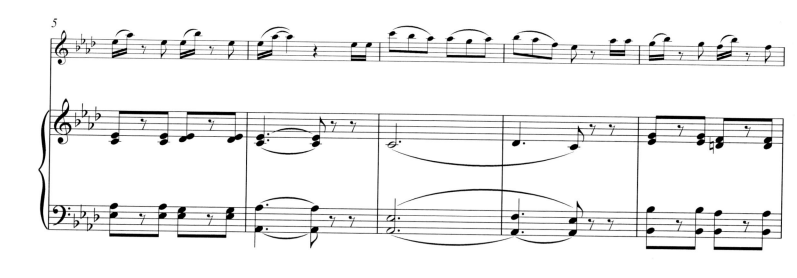

Poor Wand'ring One
from *The Pirates of Penzance*
arranged for Flute and Piano
for Sir James Galway by
David Overton

Sir Arthur Sullivan

B577

12

Take a Pair of Sparkling Eyes

from *The Gondoliers*

arranged for Flute and Piano

for Sir James Galway by

David Overton

Sir Arthur Sullivan

The Flowers that Bloom in the Spring

from *The Mikado*

arranged for Flute and Piano

for Sir James Galway by

David Overton

Sir Arthur Sullivan

Digital and photographic copying of this page is illegal.

The Sun Whose Rays

from *The Mikado*

arranged for Flute and Piano

for Sir James Galway by

David Overton

Sir Arthur Sullivan

When a Merry Maiden Marries

from *The Gondoliers*
arranged for Flute and Piano
for Sir James Galway by
David Overton

Sir Arthur Sullivan